P9-CLO-116

Berlitz®

hide this spanish book

Berlitz Publishing/APA Publications GmbH & Co. Verlag KG
Singapore Branch, Singapore

Hide This Spanish Book

Contacting the Editors
Every effort has been made to provide accurate information in this publication, but changes are inevitable. The publisher cannot be responsible for any resulting loss, inconvenience or injury. We would appreciate it if readers would call our attention to any errors or outdated information by contacting Berlitz Publishing, 193 Morris Ave., Springfield, NJ 07081, USA. Fax: 1-908-206-1103, email: comments@berlitzbooks.com

Sixth Printing: April 2006
Printed in Canada

ISBN 981-246-430-1

Writer: Isabel Mendoza
Editorial Director: Sheryl Olinsky Borg
Senior Editor: Juergen Lorenz
Editor/Project Manager: Lorraine Sova
Cover/Interior Design: Wee Design Group
Illustrator: Kyle Webster

INSIDE

THE INITIATION

Admittance to Latino culture requires more than just knowing a handful of expressions. If you really wanna get *in*, you've gotta know slang, street speak, and swear words. *Hide This Spanish Book* has what it takes so you can talk the talk. No grammar lessons, verb conjugations, or any rules here—just the language that's actually spoken in Latin America and Spain today—from the most intimate encounters (and, yeah, we're talking sex) to technology know-how (e-mail, IM, text messaging).

stuff you gotta know

It's assumed you already know a little bit of the Spanish language. Most of the expressions provided can be applied to both guys and girls. You'll see ♂ if the word or phrase can be applied to guys alone and ♀ when it's for girls only.

In case you're uncertain about how to pronounce something in the book and don't want to sound like a fool, go on-line: **www.berlitzbooks.com/hidethisbook.htm** and listen up. You may want to lower the volume...

watch out for...

We've labeled the hottest language with a thermometer, so you can easily gauge just how "bad" the expression really is. You'll see:

> These are pretty crude and crass—use with caution (or not).

> Ouch! Be very careful! Totally offensive, completely inappropriate, and downright nasty terms are labeled with this symbol.

We're dealing with real-life Spanish in this book and, therefore, we tell you what the closest English equivalent is—so you know <u>when</u> to use each word, phrase, or expression.

You'll also find these features throughout the book:

 Slang that's really vulgar or shocking

FACT   Cool facts that may seem like fiction

     Tips on what's hot and what's not

finally

You know that language is constantly changing—what's in today may be out tomorrow. So, if you come across anything in this book that's no longer said, or learn a cool expression that hasn't been included, let us know; we'd love to hear from you. Send us an email: **comments@berlitzbooks.com**. We'll add any hot new expressions to our website—go to **www.berlitzbooks.com/hidethisbook.htm** to check it out.

This book isn't labeled **Un-Censored** for nothing! This isn't the language you wanna use around your boss, relatives, or your new boy- or girlfriend's parents...got it? The stuff that's in here is pretty hot. If you wanna say it in public, that's up to you. But we are not taking the rap (like responsibility and liability) for any mistakes you make—these include, but are not limited to, verbal abuse, fist fights, smackdowns, and/or arrests that may ensue from your usage of the words and expressions in *Hide This Spanish Book*.

BASIC
EXPRESSIONS

*E*verything you need to meet and greet in Spanish.

- ◆ *say hello and good-bye*
- ◆ *ask what's up*
- ◆ *get someone's attention*

make the first move

Tired of the plain "Hola"? Try these other ways to say hello.

¿Cómo andas?
How're you doing?
Say it with a fresh, relaxed attitude.

¡Quiubo!
What's going on?
It's the shortened form of "¿Qué hubo?" Say it in one quick shot.

¡Quiay!
What's up?
This is the fast way to say "¿Qué hay?"

¿Entonces qué?
What's happening?
Use with your close friends, exclusively.

¿Qué onda?
What's up?
Very Mexican, but sounds cool everywhere.

¿Cómo van las cosas?
How's it going?
Informal, but still polite.

It is very unusual for young Latinos to shake hands when greeting or being introduced. They prefer to gently hit fists. Sometimes, a friendly glance or a slight nod is enough. Kissing on the cheek (on both cheeks for Argentineans and Spaniards) is also very common, but never between guys, with the exception of Argentineans, Chileans, and Uruguayans. In all other countries, close male friends—at the most—hug warmly, especially when they haven't seen each other for a while.

chapter 1

Un-Censored

These regional greetings can be dirty in some countries. But, in the countries below, they're the coolest ways to say hello to your friends.

¿Qué fue, cómo está la verga?
How's it hanging?
Used in Venezuela.

¿Entonces qué, marica?
What's happening, queer (sissy)?
A Colombian favorite.

¿Qué hacés, boludo?
What are you doing, big balls?
Argentina's world-famous greeting.

¡Quiubo, huevón!
What's going on, big balls?
Said in Chile.

how're ya?

The most effective way to get a conversation going is to ask someone how he or she is doing. Here are some of the best ways to ask—and answer.

– **¿Todo bien?** Is everything OK?
– **Ajá.** Yeah.

– **¿En qué andas?** What are you up to?
– **Todo lo mismo.** All the same.

– **¿Qué más de tu vida?** How's life?
– **Todo bien.** Everything's OK.

yo!

Get someone's attention using these...

¡Mira!
Look!
Just add "chica", girl, or "chico", boy, before "mira" to make it more personal.

¡Compadre! ♂ ¡Comadre! ♀
Bro! Sis!
Make someone feel like part of the family.

¡Oiga, hermano!
Hey, bro!

catch ya later!

And when it's time to go, leave your imprint by using these farewells.

Chao.
Bye.
The standard, but still the coolest way to say good-bye.

Hasta luego.
See you later.
A classic.

Me piro.
I'm out of here.
Get right to the point!

Ahí nos vemos.
See you.
It's catchy and cute.

Leave with style.

— **Bueno, me piro.** Well, I'm out of here.
— **Okay, ahí nos vemos.** OK. See you.

from HOOKING UP to BREAKING UP

*W*hether you're looking to turn on the charm or turn away an unwanted advance, have the expressions you need on the tip of your tongue.

- ◆ *come on to someone*
- ◆ *flatter and flirt like a pro*
- ◆ *deflate someone's ego*
- ◆ *reject a loser*

pick-up lines

Don't miss an opportunity to approach that guy or girl you're into because Spanish has got you tongue-tied! Practice these fool-proof pick-up lines and you're guaranteed to score.

¿Estás solo?
Are you alone?
The obvious approach—but it works every time.

¿Quieres tomar algo?
Can I buy you a drink?
Say it with sophistication.

¿Bailamos?
Shall we dance?
This one could be the beginning of a beautiful relationship.

These pick-up lines used by guys are cheesy, but they're also great for some laughs. And who knows? They may work for you!

¿Por qué tan solita?
Why are you so lonely?

¡Quiubo, mamita!
What's going on, hot lady?!

Hola, nena.
Hello, baby.

Start a conversation...

– **¿Quieres tomar algo?** Can I buy you a drink?
– **Bueno, gracias.** OK, thanks.
or
– **No, gracias.** No, thanks.

you flirt!

Is he or she hot? Say so!

Ese tipo es...   That guy is...
buen mozo.   handsome.
un papito / papacito.   hot. (Literally: a daddy)

Esa chica es...   That girl is...
una mamita / mamacita.   hot. (Literally: a mommy)
una hembra* 🌡 / hembrota. 🌡 totally hot.

Él es atractivo.
He is attractive.

Ella está divina.
She is divine.

Es un tipo muy caliente.
He's a hot guy.

Tiene buena pinta.
She is good-looking.

¡Él es un tremendo bizcocho!
He is totally cute! (Literally: He is a tremendous cupcake!)

Say it to him:

Eres...   You're...
simpático.   nice.
muy agradable.   very nice.

Say it to her:

Eres...   You're...
linda.   pretty.
guapa.   cute.
muy atractiva.   very attractive.

*Guys may talk about a girl being "una hembra" among themselves, but would never say it to a girl's face—"una hembra" is any female animal.

flat-out refusals

Reject someone like a pro. Latinos can be masters of the art of come-ons and put-downs—some even call themselves "lenguas venenosas", poisonous tongues. Be subtle or be bold—take your pick from the phrases below.

No, gracias. Estoy cansado.
No, thanks. I'm tired.
This one's pretty weak—use it and you may get talked into a date.

Estoy esperando a alguien.
I am expecting someone.
He/She can take a hint.

¡No canse!
Don't be a pain! (Literally: Don't bother [me]!)
Strong and sassy! Just the way we like it.

¡No moleste!
Don't be a pest!
A popular way to get someone to leave you alone.

No, ¿qué le pasa?
No way! What's wrong with you?
You can dish it...but can you take it?!

¡Déjeme en paz!
Leave me alone! (Literally: Leave me in peace!)
Say it like an order.

¡Lárguese!
Go away!
Not very nice, but it's crystal clear.

¡Písese! COLOMBIA
Piss off!
It's nasty, but to the point.

Looking to score? Good luck!

– **¡Eres una mamacita!** You're hot!
– **¡Déjeme en paz!** Leave me alone!

2GOOD4U

Definitely not interested? Try one of these:

¿Viste qué...es?	Did you see how...he is?
feo	ugly
maluco	gross
asqueroso	disgusting

Élla es...	She is...
un asco.	repulsive.
un cuero.	hideous. (Literally: a piece of leather)
una porquería.	filthy.

 **FACT** "Esa mujer es un cuero" usually means that woman is hideous, but in Puerto Rico it means that she's easy. And, believe it or not, Bolivian, Chilean, Mexican, and Peruvian guys may like a "cuero" because in those countries she's a pretty woman.

cheater, cheater

Nasty things to call that cheater...

Es un...	He is a...
faltón.	cheater.
sinvergüenza.	shameless guy.
perro.	cheating dog.

Ella le está poniendo los cuernos.
She is fooling around on him. (Literally: She is putting the horns on him.)

gettin' dumped

Breakin' it off with class...

Ella...	She...
le terminó.	ended it.
lo mandó a freír espárragos.	broke it off. (Literally: sent him to fry asparagus)
lo echó.	dumped him.
lo mandó pa'l carajo. 🌡	sent him to hell.
le dio una patada por el culo. 🌡	kicked his ass.

breaking up

Fallen out of love? Here are the best ways to break it off.

Seamos sólo amigos.
Let's just be friends.
Yeah, right.

Démonos un tiempo.
Let's take some time apart.
Only a coward would say this one—you know he or she really means it's over.

Ya no quiero seguir contigo.
I'm breaking up with you.
Sorry!

Esto se acabó.
It's over between us.
And this chapter too!

LOVE and SEX

Arouse your knowledge of the language of passion.

- ◆ *get romantic—from kissing to sex*
- ◆ *the best ways to say we did it*
- ◆ *gossip about virgins and sluts*
- ◆ *talk about STDs*

in the mood for love?

The expressions you need to tell your love story...

Havin' Fun

Sólo estamos vacilando.
We're just fooling around.
It's nothing serious, right?!

Tenemos un cuento.
We're just seeing each other. (Literally: We have a story.)
Meaning: we can see other people too.

Somos amigovios.
We are a pseudo-couple. (Literally: We're a friends-couple.)
A very casual relationship.

Gettin' Serious

Estamos saliendo.
We're going out.
Let everyone know!

Es mi novio.
He is my boyfriend.
In Latin America, you don't have sex with your "novio" or "novia"—at least that's the unwritten rule, which many break very quickly!

And Finally...Sex

Somos amantes.
We're lovers.
"Amantes" implies sexual activity.

hot n' heavy

It's about havin' a good time—from kissing to making love, "hacer el amor".

Bésame.
Kiss me.

Dame un beso.
Give me a kiss.

Dame un pico.
Give me a little kiss. (Literally: Peck me.)

Estoy arrecha, cariño.
I'm feeling horny, honey.

Hazme el amor.
Make love to me.

sweet talk

A common pet name in Spanish culture, "cielito lindo" literally means little pretty sky; the phrase was immortalized by a popular Mexican mariachi song. Here are some other terms of endearment you might want to try out:

Dame un beso,...	Give me a kiss,...
cariño.	honey.
mi vida.	my life.
mi amor.	my love.
mi cielo.	my sky.
mami. ♀	honey. (Literally: mommy)
papi. ♂	honey. (Literally: daddy)
gorda.	fat woman.
gordo.	fat man.
	Totally common, even among skinny people!

18

Un-Censored

And...what about sex? You'd need a whole book to learn all the dirty words and expressions used! Most of these are regional and—since the words usually have meanings that aren't sex-related, they're widely used in other countries—the chances of being embarrassed are amazingly high. Here's your basic personal defense kit:

¡Les encanta...! They love to @#&!!

chingar
Mexican—in other regions it means to joke, to get drunk, or to cut the tail of an animal.

coger
Used in Argentina, El Salvador, Guatemala, Honduras, Mexico, Nicaragua, Paraguay, Uruguay, and Venezuela. Elsewhere, it simply means to catch, to take, or to hold.

comer
Used in Chile, Colombia, Ecuador, Peru, and Venezuela. Literally means to eat.

culear
Colombian; it literally means to move the butt.

follar
Used in Spain. In other countries it means to grow leaves.

joder
Used in Spain. In other countries it means to annoy or injure.

tirar
Used in Chile, Colombia, Ecuador, Peru, and Venezuela. Anywhere else, it's defined as to throw away.

Watch out! The vulgarity level of these terms is high. Stick to the sweet "les encanta hacer el amor", they love to make love, or to the plain "les encanta tener sexo", they love to have sex, if you don't want to risk it.

countless ways to say we did it

Tuvimos relaciones sexuales.
We had sexual intercourse.
The typical medical term.

Tuvimos sexo.
We had sex.
Very plain and very cold.

Amanecimos juntos.
We woke up together.
It's a couple thing.

Pasamos la noche.
We spent the night together.
How romantic!

Dormimos juntos.
We slept together.
Doubt anyone slept...

Pasó lo que sabemos.
We know "it" happened.
Oh, yeah!

Pasó lo que tenía que pasar.
And what was supposed to happen, happened.
Ahhh, destiny.

Se puso cariñoso.
He became more and more affectionate.
How cute.

from virgin to slut

Here's how to call it like it is.

Ella es...	She's...
una niña bien.	a prissy girl. (Literally: a good girl)
una chica sana.	a nice girl. (Literally: a sane girl)
una coqueta.	a flirt.
una mosquita muerta.	a slut. (Literally: a dead fly)
una zorra.	a whore. (Literally: a fox)
una puta.	a bitch.

Él es...	He's...
un caballero.	a gentleman.
un tipo sano.	a nice guy. (Literally: a sane guy)
un tipo zanahorio.	a respectful guy. (Literally: a carrot guy)
un mujeriego.	a womanizer.
un avión.	aggressive. (Literally: an airplane)
un perro.	a player.
un vagabundo.	

Looks like someone's jealous!

– **Me gusta esa chica.** I like that girl.
– **¡Es una coqueta!** She's such a flirt!
– **Es una tipa sexy, ¡eso es todo!** She's just sexy, that's all!

the
scoop

Though many equate Latin with passion, virginity is sacred in many regions of Latin America and Spain. Traditionally, women are expected to remain chaste until marriage. This belief is still upheld—or at least proclaimed to be—by the general population. However, nowadays, a growing number of young people are sexually active long before getting married.

kinky fun

Like to party?

Compré ropa interior erótica.
I bought some erotic underwear.

Nos encanta ver películas porno.
We love to watch porno movies.

Le gustan los tríos.
He/She likes threesomes.

safe sex

Be careful! You'll probably need these:

¿Tienes...?
condones
forros (Literally: covers)
capuchas (Literally: hoods)
impermeables (Literally: raincoats)
mangas (Literally: sleeves)

Do you have <u>condoms</u>?

¿Tomas la píldora?
Are you on the pill?

Tengo el aparato / la "T".
I use an IUD.

¿Usamos espuma?
Should we use spermicide?

Espera me pongo el diafragma.
Wait! I'll put in the diaphragm.

Practice your bedside manners.

– ¿Tomas la píldora? Are you on the pill?
– ¡No! Es mejor que te pongas un forro.
No! You'd better use a condom.

STDs 101

Don't get caught with your pants down.

Le pegaron una trepadora.
She has a VD. (Literally: She has a climbing plant.)

¿Te pringaron?
Did you get infected? (Literally: Did you get greasy?)

¡Esa mujer es una venérea!
That woman has all kinds of VDs!

¿Te has hecho pruebas de venéreas?
Have you been tested for STDs?

Él/Ella tiene...	He/She has...
una enfermedad venérea.	a venereal disease.
gonorrea.	gonorrhea.
herpes.	herpes.
sida.	AIDS.
sífilis.	syphilis.

Make sure you ask...

– ¿Te has hecho la prueba del sida? Have you had an AIDS test?
– Sí. Estoy sano. Sure. I'm clean.

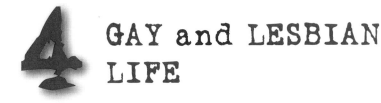

GAY and LESBIAN LIFE

*L*ooking for fun in all the alternative places? Look no further.

◆ talk about gay culture
◆ slang terms for gay guys, lesbians, and bisexuals

gay pride

Just like all other cultures, Latinos have a colorful vocabulary for unconventional lifestyles.

Juan Carlos llegó con su gatito.
Juan Carlos arrived with his young boyfriend. (Literally: Juan Carlos arrived with his kitten.)

Meow!

¡Alejandro está hecho un Simba!
Alejandro is a totally experienced gay!

"Simba" is a full-grown "gatito"; it's an analogy to a character from The Lion King.

¿Será "de ambiente"?
Do you think he's gay?

Watch out! "De ambiente" is often used to describe a person who is cheerful and likes to party, no matter what his or her sexual preferences are.

Julián nos presentó a su hembrito.
Julián introduced us to his gay partner.

"Hembrito" comes from "hembra", female animal; it's forced into the male form.

Dicen que es todo un camajo.
They say that he's a great (gay) lover.

Really?!

Andrés salió del clóset.
Andrés came out of the closet.

Oh yeah!

is he gay?

Whether you're gay or have a friend who is, here's the language you need to talk about homosexuality.

Es...

gay.

mariposo. (Literally: a butterfly)

Butterfly, which is a feminine noun, is forced into the masculine form.

roscón. (Literally: a doughnut)

voltiado. (Literally: turned over)

marica / maricón. ▌ (Literally: a fairy)

In Colombia, young people—even girls— often use this term to address their good friends, without it being offensive whatsoever.

He is <u>gay</u>.

is she a lesbian?

Es...

marimacho.

maricona.

arepera*. ▌ COLOMBIA

tortillera*. ▌ MEXICO

cachapera*. ▌ VENEZUELA

She is a <u>lesbian</u>.

Warning! If used in the wrong context, all of these terms can be derogatory.

*All of these literally mean: a woman who makes corncakes.

is he or she bi?

Ella juega a los dos bandos.
She swings both ways. (Literally: She plays on both teams.)

Él es de doble tracción.
He is of double traction.
It refers to the front- and rear-wheel drive of a car.

 Though homosexuality is still taboo in Spain and many Latin American countries, its legitimacy is beginning to be recognized by more and more people. Gay activism is a part of alternative culture for Latinos; this has helped spread awareness and prevent discrimination.

SPORTS and GAMES

*F*rom the stadium to the gym, on the field or behind the joystick, don't
let anybody make sport of your Spanish.

- ◆ cheer for your team and insult the opposition
- ◆ talk about soccer—because Latinos love to
- ◆ work up a sweat about gym language
- ◆ toy around with video-game lingo
- ◆ get in on the gambling action

cheers

Hey sports fans—"hinchas / aficionados"—motivate the players with these.

¡A ganar!
Go for it!
Shout it out loud and raise both arms.

¡Arriba ese ánimo!
Cheer up!
Share some words of encouragement.

¡Sí se puede!
It's doable!
Show your undying support.

¡Estamos vivos!
Still alive!
Is your favorite team losing? Try this first-aid cry.

¡Duro con ellos!
Show no mercy! (Literally: Be rude to them!)

¡Métasela duro!
Give it to them! (Literally: Stick it hard!)
The opposition must suffer!

¡Goléenlos!
Beat them! (Literally: Fill them with goals!)

¡Hágale!
Go!
Scream it at the top of your lungs.

¡Dele!
Go for it!

¡Vamos!
Come on! / Let's go!
There's no time to lose!

¡Gol!
Goal!

compliments

Use these expressions to celebrate your team's spectacular moves and shots.

¡Qué jugada tan...!	It was a/an...move!
hermosa	beautiful
excelsa	sublime
magnífica	magnificent
macanuda ARGENTINA	extraordinary
sobrada COLOMBIA	out-of-this-world

¡Qué golazo!
What a winner! (Literally: Great goal!)

¡Qué partidazo!
What a game!

¡García se sobró!
Garcia was out of this world!

¡Sánchez barrió con la defensa del América!
Sanchez wiped the floor with América's defense!

If you don't know it already, "America" is Colombia's famed soccer team.

Never make the mistake of confusing "football" with "fútbol" in front of a Latino. When Latinos say "fútbol" they are not talking about American football—they're talking about soccer. In Spanish, American football is "fútbol americano". And don't dare to contradict them—"fútbol" is sacred and is taken very seriously.

insults

Harassing the referee, "árbitro", humiliating the opponent, "contrincante", and judging your team, "equipo", is part of your job as a spectator.

¡Pítele!
Foul! (Literally: Whistle at him!)

¡Sáquelo!
Kick him out!
Say it with anger.

¡Vendido!
You took a bribe! (Literally: Paid for!)
Don't worry; you won't be sued for slander.

¡Malditos!
Damn!

¡Les va la madre!
Your mother wears army boots!
It may seem corny, but this is a pretty nasty putdown.

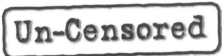

Un-Censored

A soccer game is the perfect scenario to use all the dirty words that you know. Here is a good selection; we suggest you use them inside the stadium only!

¡Hijueputa!
Son of a bitch!

¡Coño de tu madre!
Your mom's ass!

¡Cabrones!
Bastards! (Literally: Billy goats!)

¡Chinga tu madre! MEXICO
@#&! your mother!

¡Vaya por la puta bola!
Go get the @#&!ing ball!

more abuse

Judge your team—and the opposing one—fair and square.

¡Así no es!
What the hell is that!
Say it to the player who obviously knows nothing about the game.

¡Pónganse las pilas!
Get it on! (Literally: Put the batteries on!)
This must sound demanding.

¡Animal! 🌡
Asshole! (Literally: Animal!)
Scream this when the player is acting beastly.

¡Imbéciles!
¡Chingaos! MEXICO ⎤ Jerks!

¡Bruto! 🌡
Idiot! (Literally: Stupid!)
Believe or not, this is rather polite, considering some of the alternatives.

¡Mucha señorita!
You throw like a girl! (Literally: What a Miss!)
Hey! Girls also know how to play soccer.

¡Chimbo! VENEZUELA, COLOMBIA
¡Chafa! MEXICO ⎤ Cheap!

¡Huevón! 🌡
¡Boludo! 🌡 ARGENTINA ⎤ Got balls!
Consider these two of many ruthless ways to say:
You can do better, buddy.

 Hooliganism is not a widespread phenomenon in Latino culture. In general, people are very passionate about sports but remain polite at the stadium. However, some take their passion for soccer so seriously that rivalry between fans of opposing teams can easily become a personal matter. Jokes can turn into offenses and friendships can be jeopardized by a humiliating comment. Famous wins, "goleadas", literally, *feasts of goals*, remain in people's memories so long that even a slight reminder of a shameful loss can turn into a personal offense years later.

got game?

There's more to life than just soccer.

¿Te gusta...?	Do you like...?
el béisbol	baseball
el básquetbol	basketball
el boxeo	boxing
el automovilismo	car racing
el ciclismo	cycling
la pelota vasca	jai alai
el rugby	rugby
el monopatín	skateboarding
el atletismo	track and field
el voleibol	volleyball
el levantamiento de pesas	weightlifting
la lucha libre	free-style wrestling

The most popular extreme sports among Latino youth are cyclocross, "ciclocross" (it's serious cycling, over rough terrain at fast speeds); motocross, "motocross" (it's just like cyclocross, but with a motorcycle); mountain biking, "ciclomontañismo"; and mountain climbing, "escalada". Dare to give them a try?

working out

It's all about a hot body!

Vamos...	Let's...
al gimnasio.	go to the gym.
a hacer ejercicio.	exercise.
a hacer aeróbicos.	do aerobics.
a entrenar.	train.
a hacer pesas.	work out with weights.
a hacer máquinas.	work out with machines.

¡Esfuérzate!
Make an effort!

¡Ponte un reto!
Challenge yourself!

¡Me agota!
It's exhausting!

Estoy completamente...	I'm totally...
rendido.	exhausted.
mamado. COLOMBIA	
hecho polvo.	pulverized.
acabado.	run-down.
agotado / molido.	worn-out. (Literally: ground)

¡Estoy sudando a chorros!
The sweat is pouring out of me!

Estoy dolorido.
I feel stiff.

Tengo agujetas. SPAIN
I'm sore.

machinery & more

Pump some iron and get into shape.

Hoy hice...	Today I worked on...
spinning.	the spinner.
escaladora.	the stair climber.
caminadora.	the treadmill.
¿Tienen...en este gimnasio?	Do you have...in this gym?
sauna	a sauna
baño turco	a steam room
masajes	massage service
No olvides tu...	Don't forget your...
bicicletero / lycras.	bike shorts.
trusa y malla.	leotard and leggings.
sudadera.	sweatsuit.
toalla.	towel.

Who's the real sports enthusiast?

– **¡Me encanta el spinning!** I love spinning!
– **Prefiero hacer aeróbicos.** I like aerobics better.

In Latin America, gyms grow more popular everyday, and it's not only because people want to look and feel good. Fitness centers have become the place to relax and socialize. For many Latinos, the gym is definitely a hot spot to make friends with cute people.

fun n' games

*If you're a video game aficionado, you'll feel at ease with Spanish games—
many of the terms used are in English. They even have English terms to
name game tools, equipment, and commands.*

¿Vamos a jugar un rato con el play?
Want to play with PlayStation®?

¿Jugamos cube?
Want to play GameCube™?

¿Apretaste el botón de encendido?
Did you press the power button?

Pásame el joystick.
Hand me the joystick.

Apúntale al monstruo verde.
Aim at the green monster.

¡Le di!
I hit it!

¡Me lo bajé!
I knocked it down!

¡Lo quemé!
I burned it!

¡Lo maté!
I killed it!

*Big cities throughout Latin America are full of arcades and, since most young
people don't have electronic games at home, arcades are usually crowded
seven days a week. Hint: These are great places to socialize and make friends.*

gambling

Even if you think Lady Luck is on your side, play it safe and practice these expressions before you put your money down and risk it all.

Hagan sus apuestas.
Place your bets.

Le apuesto 200 pesos al 5.
I'll bet 200 pesos on number 5.

¡Gané!
I won!

¡Me saqué la lotería!
I won the lotto!

¡Me han estafado! / ¡Me tumbaron!
I've been scammed!

Estoy salado.
I'm never lucky. (Literally: I'm salted.)

 In many countries, gambling in casinos, social clubs, racetracks, and stadiums is prohibited for those under 18. However, arcades usually have *slot machines*, "tragamonedas" or "tragaperras" (Spain), which are often played by teens. People under 18 can also gamble in arcades for minors only. You don't win money, but you do get more tokens to continue playing, or tickets that can be exchanged for items such as stuffed toys, posters, stationery, or CDs.

 # SHOPPING

Get ready to shop till you drop.

- ◆ *shop like a pro*
- ◆ *make a deal and bargain with the best of 'em*

let's go shopping!

Grab your wallet along with this essential list of shopper's questions.

¿Dónde está la sección de...?   Where's the...department?
damas / caballeros   women's / men's
ropa deportiva   sportswear
trajes de baño   swimwear
zapatos   shoe
cosméticos   cosmetics

¿Lo tienen en la talla 10?
Do you have it in size 10?

¿En qué otros colores lo tienen?
What other colors do you have?

¿Dónde queda el vestier?
Where's the fitting room?

¿Tienen otros estilos?
Do you have other styles?

¿Dónde puedo encontrar...?   Where can I find...?
CDs
Ce-des SPAIN ⎤   CDs
DVDs
De-uve-des SPAIN ⎤   DVDs
postales   postcards
libros   books
revistas   magazines

Besides department stores, in Latin America you'll come across shopping centers with kiosks where you can find new, cool stuff. In general, these are *contraband* products, "contrabando". In the "mercados de las pulgas", *flea markets*, you can find used goods and other bargains. Costa Rican "chinamos" and Mexican "changarros" are also *flea markets*. You'll find handcrafted items at farmer's markets.

sales q & a

What did that sales clerk just say? You might have heard...

¿A la orden? CENTRAL AMERICA

¿Para servirle? LATIN AMERICA   Can I help you?

¿En qué puedo ayudarle? SPAIN

¿Qué talla busca?
What size are you looking for?

¿Cuál es su talla?
What is your size?

Shoo away that annoying sales clerk.

– **¿Para servirle?** Can I help you?
– **Sólo estoy mirando, gracias.** I'm just
looking, thanks.

pay up!

Looking to part with your hard-earned dough? Here's the lingo you need to make your purchase.

¿Cuánto cuesta?
How much does it cost?

¿Tiene descuento?
Is it on sale?

¿Puedo pagar con tarjeta de crédito?
Can I pay by credit card?

No se fía.
No layaway given.

money, money, money

Different ways to say cash...

¿Tienes...que me prestes?
dinero
plata ARGENTINA
quivo BOLIVIA
tuco CARIBBEAN
billullo COLOMBIA
cañas COSTA RICA
baros CUBA
billuzo ECUADOR
lana MEXICO
riales VENEZUELA
guita SPAIN

Can you lend me
some <u>cash</u>?

Different ways to say change...

No tengo...
cambio.
cambio chico. ARGENTINA
menudo. CENTRAL AMERICA
sencillo. COLOMBIA
cacharpa. MEXICO
calderilla. SPAIN

I don't have <u>change</u>.

Every country has its own slang to talk about local currency. In Argentina and Peru, pesos are known informally as "mangos". Bolivian and Colombian "lucas" is a slang term for bolivianos and pesos, respectively. And "durantes" is the favorite term for pesos in the Dominican Republic.

it's a steal

You can bank on success with these bargain expressions.

¿Dónde hay ventas de bodega?
Where are the outlet stores?

¡Hay rebajas todo el fin de semana!
There is a sale all weekend!

Los relojes están en rebaja.
The watches are on sale.

¡Esto es una verdadera ganga!
This is a real bargain!

¿Es ése el precio final?
Is that the final price?

Le ofrezco 500 pesos.
I'll give you 500 pesos.

Esta bufanda me salió...
gratis.
gratarola. ARGENTINA   I got this scarf for <u>free</u>.
de a grapa. MEXICO

Feel free to bargain at any flea market, small mom n' pop stores, farmer's markets, and with street vendors who offer accessories and services just for tourists. If you tip the bartender handsomely early on, you may be able to score free drinks towards the end of your drinking session. Don't bargain in supermarkets and department stores—it won't work.

 Can't find your size? That's because clothing and shoe sizes in Latin America can vary from country to country. You'll find S, M, L, and XL for both men and women in Argentina, Chile, Colombia, Ecuador, Mexico, Spain, Uruguay, and Venezuela. P, XS, and XXL are very rare—petite women should try the *children's department*, "Niños" or "Infantil", or *juniors' department*, "Jóvenes".

Numbers can also be used to indicate size. Ladies—Use this table to figure out what will fit you best.

US	Spain	Colombia
XS	32 and 34	6
S	36	8
M	38 and 40	10
L	42 and 44	12
L	46 and 48	14
L	50 and 52	16
XL	54 and 56	18
XXL	58	20 and 22

Guys—Looking for jeans? In Spain and Latin America, sizes are labeled as in the US.

What about shoes? Don't fret! US sizes apply in Argentina, Ecuador, Mexico, and Venezuela. But, some shoe stores, mainly in Colombia and Chile, apply a different numbering system: just add 30 to your normal US shoe size and keep in mind that half sizes aren't available.*

Women's US Sizes	Women's Latin American Sizes
6	36
7	37
8	38
9	39
10	40

Men's US Sizes	Men's Latin American Sizes
9	39
10	40
11	41
12	42
13	43

Sizes may vary.

FASHION

*S*lip into this chic chapter and learn how to look and sound totally
Spanish.

- ◆ gossip about fashion dos and don'ts
- ◆ name all the clothes in your ultra chic wardrobe
- ◆ pay some lip service to make-up
- ◆ prep for a good hair day
- ◆ enhance your knowledge of body alterations

ready to wear

Looks aren't everything—you've also got to be fashion forward in Spanish!

Estos pantalones...	These pants...
están en pleno furor.	are all the rage this season.
son el último grito de la moda.	are the latest thing.
están "in" / "out".	are in / out.
están pasados de moda.	are old-fashioned.

Te ves bien con esa pinta.
That's a good look for you.

Melissa...	Melissa...
está a la moda.	is fashionable.
está pintosa. COLOMBIA	dresses fashionably.
se ve arriba de la bola. CUBA	looks great.
viste muy catrina. MEXICO	dresses very elegantly.

Manuel es un gallo. ♂
Manuel is very elegant. (Literally: Manuel is a rooster.)

fashion no-no

Got a friend without fashion sense? Make sure he knows it!

¡Daniel se viste...!	Daniel is a...dresser!
adrenalítico CHILE	flashy
lobo COLOMBIA	gaudy
huachafo PERU	tacky
como un croto ARGENTINA	crappy (Literally: like a beggar)

what's in your closet?

Show off your knowledge of the right Spanish attire.

un brasier
un sujetador SPAIN ⎤ bra

una blusa escotada
halter top

una tanga
bikini

un vestido de baño
swimsuit

una falda
skirt

un brasier con relleno
padded bra

una tanga brasi-lera
thong

unos tenis
sneakers

unas pantuflas
unas zapatillas SPAIN ⎤ slippers

unos calzones
unas bragas SPAIN ⎤ panties

46

una chaqueta
jacket

unos yins
unos vaqueros SPAIN jeans

unas gafas
glasses

una gorra
baseball cap

una camiseta
t-shirt

una mochila
backpack

unos calzon-cillos
briefs

un suéter
sweater

unas sandalias
sandals

make your beauty mark

Apply these beauty expressions and you'll look—and sound—good.

¿Me prestas un poco de...?	Can I borrow some...?
maquillaje	make-up
polvorete	blush
delineador	eyeliner
sombras	eye shadow
pintalabios	lipstick
rimel	mascara
polvos	powder
Por favor, necesito...	Please, I need...
un pincel fino.	a make-up brush.
un encrespador de pestañas.	an eyelash curler.
un pomo.	a powder puff.
una esponja.	a sponge.
unas pinzas para depilar.	tweezers.

pamper yourself

Go ahead and indulge in a Spanish spa experience.

Quisiera...	I'd like...
un masaje facial.	a facial.
hacerme un manicure.	a manicure.
hacerme un pedicure.	a pedicure.
un masaje.	a massage.
depilarme el área del bikini.	a bikini wax.
depilarme las cejas.	my eyebrows waxed.

let your hair down

From cut to curls, find the language you need to get the hairstyle you want.

¿Dónde hay un salón de belleza bueno?
Where's a good salon?

Quiero teñirme el pelo.
I want to dye my hair.

Quiero hacerme iluminaciones.
I want some highlights.

¿Dónde hay una barbería?
Where's the barbershop?

Necesito cortarme el pelo.
I need a hair cut.

Me gusta ese chico...	I like that boy with the...
de cabello rizado.	curly hair.
pelinegro.	black hair.
rubio.	blonde hair.
de pelo castaño.	brown hair.
pelirrojo.	red hair.

A short, classic cut for men and a straight, classy hairstyle for women is the standard look in most Latin American countries. When it comes to hair trends, chic people in Latin America and Spain follow current American styles—bright, unconventional colors and wet-looking tresses have been all the rage. Although hip hairstyles are OK for college students, funky locks are by no means accepted in most schools or workplaces.

wash up

Don't forget those toiletry essentials! Keep your language fresh and clean.

Just for him...

¿Dónde puedo comprar...?	Where can I buy...?
crema de afeitar	shaving cream
loción para después de la afeitada	aftershave lotion
gel para el pelo	hair gel
una loción fina / una colonia	cologne

Just for her...

¿Me regalas...?	Can I have...?
una compresa	a pad
un tampón	a tampon
crema de manos	some hand lotion
un poco de perfume	some perfume

body alterations

Fashion is more than just the right clothes. You've got to have the right body too.

¿Te has hecho alguna cirugía plástica?
Did you have plastic surgery?

Me arreglé...	I had...
los senos.	a boob job.
la nariz.	a nose job.
la barbilla.	chin augmentation.

Se infló...	She enhanced her...
las tetas.	boobs.
las nalgas.	butt.
los labios.	lips.
Se hizo...	She got...
el tummy tuck.	a tummy tuck.
la lipo.	liposuction.
el maquillaje permanente.	permanent make-up.

Se estiró la cara.
She had a face lift.

Uso botox.
I use botox.

Él tiene un piercing en...	He has a/an...piercing.
el ombligo.	belly button
una ceja.	eyebrow
un pezón.	nipple
la nariz.	nose

¡Qué tatuaje más chévere!
That tattoo is cool!

Popular body alterations among Latino teens include piercings, tattoos, and several types of esthetic surgery. In some Latin American countries, youngsters pierce their body just like their peers in the US and Europe. In Colombia, Venezuela, Argentina, and Spain, girls undergo plastic surgery from as early as at the age of 14 or 15, usually to increase the size of their breasts or buttocks, to flatten the tummy, to reduce the thighs or hips, or to embellish features such as the nose, lips, or chin. Permanent make-up is also popular among Latino young ladies.

 **BODY**

*T*he bare facts—from head to toe.

- ◆ speak up about body parts and body image
- ◆ let loose—talk about burping, farting, and other gross stuff

body beautiful

Here's the skinny on that perfect—or not-so-perfect—Latino body.

Carolina tiene...	Carolina has...
un cuerpo escultural.	a sculpted body.
buenas tetas.	nice boobs.
tremendo culo.	a great butt.
unas nalgas divinas.	an amazing butt.
buenas piernas.	nice legs.
Andrés tiene...	Andrés has...
buenas pompis.	a nice ass.
un super cuerpo.	a great body.
brazos macizos.	strong arms.
buenos pectorales.	nice pecs.
un buen bulto.	a good package.
Hernán...	Hernán...
tiene una panza / una barriga.	has a big belly.
tiene algunos rollitos.	has lovehandles.
es bajito.	is short.
es mueco.	has some teeth missing.

María está cuadrada. ♀

María is shapeless. (Literally: María is square-shaped.)

Ana nada de espalda y nada de pecho. ♀

Ana is flat, back and front. (Literally: Ana swims the backstroke and breaststroke.)

"Nada" means swim, but it also means nothing.

skin problems

Beauty is skin deep.

¡Qué desastre! Tengo...	What a disaster! I have...
un barro.	a pimple.
espinillas.	blackheads.
un callo.	a corn.
chucha. COLOMBIA	stinky armpits.
pie de atleta.	smelly feet.

¡Dios santo, cúbrete!
¿Qué haces...?
desnudo
chulón CENTRAL AMERICA
empeloto COLOMBIA
chingo COSTA RICA
bichi MEXICO
calato PERU
en pelotas SPAIN

My God! Cover yourself!
What are you doing <u>naked</u>?

body functions

Ew! Disgusting! Here's how they say it in Spanish.

Voy a orinar.
I am going to urinate.

Voy a hacer pipí / chichí.
I am going to pee.

Voy a mear.
I am going to piss.

Voy a hacer del cuerpo.
I'm going to poop. (Literally: I am going to do of the body.)

Voy a hacer número dos.
I am going to do number two.

Voy a hacer popó.
I am going to poop.

Voy a hacer caca.
I am going to crap.

Voy a cagar.
I am going to shit.

gross!

Guaranteed to make you feel nauseated...

¡Alguien se tiró un pedo / un gas!
Someone farted!

¡Ernesto eructó como un chancho!
Ernesto burped like a piggy!

¡Guácala! Tienes un moco en la nariz.
Ew! You have a snot in your nose.

Tienes legañas.
You have goo in your eyes.

¡Qué asco! No te apretes las espinillas.
That's gross! Don't squeeze those blackheads.

Ese tipo tiene aliento de dragón / de alcantarilla.
That guy has dragon / drain breath.

Be tactful.

– Tienes un moco en la nariz. You have a snot in your nose.

– ¡Uy, qué vergüenza! Oh! How embarrassing!

– No hay problema. It's no big deal.

need a remedy?

Not feeling well? Try some of these...

¡Ay! Tengo...	Ugh! I have...
estreñimiento / constipación.	constipation.
diarrea.	diarrhea.
mareo.	motion sickness.
dolor de estómago.	stomach pains.
retorcijones.	cramps.
resaca.	a hangover.
cólicos menstruales.	menstrual cramps.
tos.	a cough.
fiebre / calentura.	a fever.

¡Me estoy muriendo!
I feel like crap! (Literally: I'm dying!)

¡Estoy de muerte!
I'm sick as a dog! (Literally: I'm close to death!)

¡Estás cadavérico!
You look like shit! (Literally: You look cadaverous!)

 If you're about to go out for a night on the town, but don't want to suffer with a hangover the next day, try this Latino concoction before you start drinking (there's no guarantee this will work for everyone): Swallow two tablespoons of olive oil then two tablespoons of sugar. Follow with a big glass of water. Now you're ready to party!

If preventive care isn't you're style, and you've already drunk too many tropical cocktails, here are some remedies for that "resaca", "cruda" (Mexico), or "guayabo" (Colombia), *hangover*. After reading them, you may decide that you might as well put up with the hangover...

Remedy 1: Rub each armpit with half a lemon.

Remedy 2: Blend a cup of chopped pineapple, with a cup of artichoke hearts, and enough olive oil to minimize the chunkiness. Swallow as fast as possible.

Remedy 3: Make an infusion of eggplant and sugar: cut up one medium-sized raw eggplant into cubes and coat with a lot of sugar. Add water and heat until it boils for about five minutes. Allow the mixture to sit for an hour. Drink the juice and discard the rest.

Remedy 4: Blend two raw eggs with pepper, salt, and vinegar. Drink it down in one shot.

Remedy 5: Pour yourself a glass of tomato juice and then swallow one lamb's eye soaked in vinegar. (Some ingredients may be hard to find!)

TECHNOLOGY

*C*ompute Spanish technology talk with ease.

- ◆ *process computer lingo and netspeak*
- ◆ *communicate by e-mail, IM, and in chat rooms*
- ◆ *learn how to phone your friends*
- ◆ *use text messaging shorthand*

log on

A little tech talk in Spanish.

Prende la computadora. LATIN AMERICA / **Enciende el ordenador.** SPAIN
Turn on the computer.

¿Puedo conectarme en tu PC?
Can I connect [to the internet] on your PC?

¿Puedo revisar mi correo electrónico?
Can I check my e-mail?
The English term "e-mail" is also widely used in Spanish.

¿Puedo bajar música?
Can I download music?

Estoy navegando por la Web.
I'm surfing the web.

Comprime ese archivo.
Compress that file.

Abre el documento.
Open the document.

Cierra el programa.
Close the program.

Arrastra el documento hasta la papelera.
Drag the document to the trash.

 Looking for some IT help?

– **No puedo chequear* mi e-mail.** I can't check my e-mail.
– **Déjame ayudarte.** I'll help you.
– **Uy, sí, chévere. ¡Gracias!** Cool! Thanks!

** "Chequear" is a Spanglish term, now used in much of Latin America. The official term,
which would be understood everywhere—including Spain—is "revisar".*

e-mail

Need that Spanish e-mail screen translated? No problem.

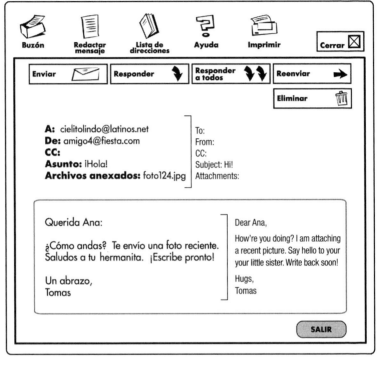

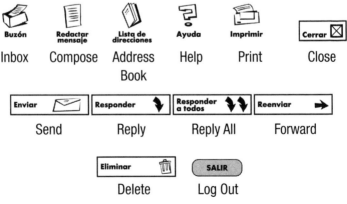

Inbox   Compose   Address   Help   Print   Close
                   Book

Send   Reply   Reply All   Forward

Delete   Log Out

help desk

Uh-oh. Facing some computer problems? These expressions could help.

Este aparato...	This machine...
se bloqueó.	
se congeló.	froze.
se quedó colgado. SPAIN	
se quedó ahí.	doesn't respond. (Literally: stayed there)
Esta cosa...	This thing...
se dañó.	got damaged.
se funó. CHILE	broke.
se desmadró. MEXICO	got screwed up. (Literally: got motherless)
se jodió. COLOMBIA	got @#&!ed up.

Tienes que reiniciar.
You have to restart it.

Many people in Latin America and Spain who don't have personal computers visit Internet cafés, where they check their e-mail and chat. Some of these cafés are cool places to meet Internet-savvy friends and foreigners while enjoying light refreshments, including popular specialty coffees and desserts.

communicate on-line

E-mail or chat in Spanish...

Me encanta ese sitio.
I love that website.
You'll also see the English word, "website", used on Spanish sites.

Esa es mi página web favorita.
That's my favorite webpage.

Mándame ese enlace.
Send me that link.

¿Cuál es tu seudónimo?
What's your ID?

¡Me encanta chatear!
I love to chat!

Dame tu e-mail / tu dirección electrónica.
Give me your e-mail / (e-mail) address.

¡No mires mi contraseña!
Don't look at my password!

Looking for some on-line lovin'? Romance rooms are among the most popular.
If you'd like to get hot and heavy on-line, you should know these phrases:

Soy una chica / un chico...	**que busca chica / chico / chica o chico...**
I'm a girl / guy.	who is looking for a girl / guy / a girl or guy...
que tenga entre XX y XX años...	**que viva en (ciudad / provincia / país)...**
who is from XX to XX years old...	who lives in (city / state / country)...
a quien le guste (pasatiempos).	**Envíame un correo a...**
who likes (hobbies).	E-mail me at...

chat room talk

When visiting a chat room, "canales de charla" or "salas de charla", keep in mind these abbreviations and expressions.

Komotás? (¿Cómo estás?)
How are you doing?
No need to use opening "?" and "!" in a Spanish chat.

nonetás? (¿Dónde estás?)
Where are you?

akatoy (Acá estoy.)
Here I am.

Ke kieres? (¿Qué quieres?)
What do you want?
Typing "k" is faster than typing "qu"... and more fun!

Ya te vas?
Are you leaving?

xk kieres irte ya? (¿Por qué quieres irte ya?)
Why do you want to leave now?
Well, maybe you're bored...

Nos pasamos a un privado?
Wanna go to a private chat room?
Need some alone time?!

Grax! (¡Gracias!)
Thnx! (Thanks!)

De nax! (¡De nada!)
You're welcome!

NPI
I have no idea.
This is an acronym for "no poseo información", I don't have the information, and "ni puta idea"; literally, I don't have a bitch clue.

instant messaging

Reach out and IM someone!

MENSAJE INSTANTÁNEO - Cielitolindo ⬓ ⬜ ✕

Cielitolindo: Hola! Komotás?
Maria0817: Hola! Recibí tu foto. Grax!
Cielitolindo: De nax!
Maria0817: k sabes de Ángel?
Cielitolindo: NPI

☺

Bloquear	Añadir amigo	Hablar	Información	Enviar
Block	Add Buddy	Talk	Get info	Send

Instant Message	Spanish Equivalent	English Translation
Hola! Komotás?	¡Hola! ¿Cómo estás?	Hi! How are you doing?
Hola! Recibi tu foto. Grax!	¡Hola! Recibí tu foto. ¡Gracias!	Hi! I got your picture. Thanks!
De nax!	¡De nada!	You're welcome!
k sabes de Ángel?	¿Qué sabes de Ángel?	What's going on with Angel?
NPI	Ni puta idea.	I have no idea.

pick it up!

Is the phone ringing? Want to call someone? Don't freak out! Learn these.

¿Dónde está el celular?
Where's the cell phone?

¿Hola?
Hello?

¿Aló?
Hi?

¿Sí?
Yes?

¿Diga?
Yes? (Literally: Say?)

¿Bueno? MEXICO
Yes? (Literally: Good?)

Hola, habla Lola.
Hello, this is Lola.
"Habla" is used in Latin America; "soy" is said in Spain.

¿Podría pasarme a Miguel por favor?
May I please speak with Miguel?

¿Está Rosa?
Is Rosa there?

Con ella habla.
Speaking. (Literally: You're talking to her.)

Un momento.
Hold on.

¿Podría pasarme a Orlando, por favor?
May I talk to Orlando, please?

Soy yo.
It's me.

¡Márcame!
Call me! (Literally: Dial me!)

¡Dame un timbrazo / un toque! SPAIN
Ring me!

get off the phone!

Learn your phone manners and hang up with grace.

Me tengo que ir.
Gotta go.

Tengo que colgar.
I have to hang up.

Llámame más tarde.
Call me later.

Mándame un beso antes de colgar.
Send me a kiss before hanging up.

What to expect on an answering machine...
– ¡Hola! Habla Isa. Al tono por favor deje un mensaje.
Hi! This is Isa. At the beep, please leave a message.
– Habla Luis. ¡Llámame! This is Luis. Call me!

text messaging

These are some popular text messaging lines. Make a note.

¿Dónde andas?
Where have you been?

Llama a casa.
Call home.

¡Llámame!
Call me!

50538 50538
Kisses, Kisses

It reads "BESOS, BESOS" when you turn the wireless phone upside down.

TQM
I love you so much.

It's the acronym for "Te quiero mucho."

MAPTC [Me apetece...]
I feel like...

What are you in the mood for...?

QTPRC [Qué te parece?]
What do you think?

Wireless phones are very popular in Latin America and Spain, but the service is usually very expensive, so people use them in moderation. Pre-paid plans or cards are used more frequently. In some countries, calling to a wireless phone has an extra charge for the caller, so making calls can get expensive. In many cases, lines are blocked so only select family and friends can make a call to the phone.

 GOSSIP

*W*hat to say, good and bad, about friends and family.

◆ gossip about people you love and hate
◆ learn to keep secrets
◆ talk about your family
◆ insult someone's mother

best of friends

Have you met some really cool people? Spread the news.

¡Qué divina!
What a sweetheart!

Él tiene un gran corazón.
He's got a big heart.

Ella es buenísima gente.
She's such a nice person.

Me cae muy bien.
I really like him.

Eres un encanto.
You're a doll.

i hate them!

Share your thoughts about those annoying acquaintances.

¡Odio a los hijos de papi!
I hate momma's boys! (Literally: I hate daddy's boys!)

Ana me cae gorda.
I don't like Ana. (Literally: Ana falls fat on me.)

Él me cae de madre. MEXICO
I don't like him. (Literally: He falls to the mother on me.)

Ese tipo es un don nadie.
That guy is a nobody. (Literally: That guy is a Mr. Nobody.)

Él es un veneno. CUBA
He is a hypocrite. (Literally: He's poison.)

¡Me pone los pelos de punta!
He gets on my nerves!

gossip

*Master the art of gossiping in Spanish. Here are the top ways to start
some good "chisme" (really juicy gossip)...*

Aquí entre nos.
It's between us.

¡Te tengo una bomba!
I have a real bomb!

¡No me lo vas a creer!
You won't believe it!

¡Agárrate!
Hold yourself tight!

¿Te enteraste de la última?
Did you hear the latest news?

keep it confidential

Go ahead, confide in your friends—just make sure your secrets remain untold.

¡Chito!
Shhh!

¡No se lo cuentes a nadie!
Don't tell.

Guárdatelo.
Keep it quiet.

¿Puedes guardar un secreto?
Can you keep a secret?

Llévatelo a la tumba.
Take it to the tomb / grave.

spreading rumors

Pointing out the faults of your enemies—or friends—is an entertaining pastime!

Ana es...	Ana is...
de la plebea.	a commoner.
una concheta. ARGENTINA	
una gomela. COLOMBIA	a daddy's girl.
una chancletera. CUBA, MEXICO	
una jíbara.	a peasant.
una niña pija. SPAIN	a snooty girl.
de alcurnia.	a stuck-up girl. (Literally: of noble lineage)

Ella es...	She is...
maliciosa.	bitchy.
una engreída.	conceited.
una apestosa.	skanky.

Él es un...	He's...
tarado.	a moron.
gil / pasmado. CENTRAL AMERICA	
buey. ♂ (Literally: an ox) MEXICO	dumb.
lenteja. (Literally: a lentil) PERU, COLOMBIA	
idiota.	an idiot.
boludo. ARGENTINA	
gilipollas. SPAIN	a jerk.
huevón. (Literally: big balls)	a fool.

Santiago es...	
maldoso. CENTRAL AMERICA	
un punto. CUBA	
un parejero. DOMINICAN REPUBLIC	Santiago is a <u>nasty guy</u>.
un canijo. MEXICO	
un guillú. PUERTO RICO	

71

shut up!

How do you get someone to stop bullshitting? Try these.

No seas...   Don't be such a...
mentiroso.   liar.
hablamierda. 🌡   bullshitter. (Literally: shit-speaker)

No te hagas el gil conmigo. ARGENTINA
Don't play dumb with me.

No hables paja. COLOMBIA
Don't bullshit. (Literally: Don't speak straw.)

No eches botana. MEXICO
Don't bullshit. (Literally: Don't throw snacks.)

temper, temper

Pissed off at someone? Get the anger out.

Estoy que lo mato.
I'm gonna kill him.

Estoy que reviento de la ira.
I'm about to explode with anger.

¡No me la soporto!
I can't stand her!

¡Me saca de quicio!
She pisses me off!

soothers

Got a friend who's in a bad way? Offer some words of comfort.

Cálmate. No vale la pena.
Calm down. It isn't worth the worry.

No le pares bolas.
Don't pay attention to him. (Literally: Don't fix your eyeballs on him.)

Un-Censored

Typical teases...

¡Sabelotodo!
Smart ass!

Pobre imbecil.
You poor little imbecile.

¡Huevon! / **¡Huevoncito!**
Big balls! / Little big balls!

Eres un comemierda.
You're a shithead. (Literally: You're a shit-eater.)

...And the best comebacks.

Ábrase. COLOMBIA
Get the hell out of here. (Literally: Open up.)

Púdrete.
Go rot in hell. (Literally: Rot yourself.)

¡La tuya!
Yours!

¡Vete pa' la mierda!
Go to hell! (Literally: Go to the shit.)

Me importa un culo.
I don't give a shit. (Literally: I care an ass.)

family slang

Just chillin' with your friends and want to use some Spanish words to talk about your family? Try these.

Mi...es un gran tipo.

viejo

tata COSTA RICA, GUATEMALA

taita COLOMBIA, DOMINICAN REPUBLIC

pai DOMINICAN REPUBLIC, PUERTO RICO

apá MEXICO

cocho / teclo PERU

My <u>dad</u> is a great guy.

Adoro a mi...

vieja.

tata. COSTA RICA

nana. GUATEMALA

mai. DOMINICAN REPUBLIC, PUERTO RICO

amá. MEXICO

cocha / tecla. PERU

I love my <u>mom</u>.

Wanna talk about someone's bratty child? Here are the best slang terms for kid...

chichí CENTRAL AMERICA

chaval SOUTHERN SOUTH AMERICA

guagua BOLIVIA, PERU

sardino COLOMBIA, COSTA RICA

chamaco CUBA, MEXICO

chamo CARIBBEAN, MEXICO

güiro GUATEMALA

crío SPAIN

botija URUGUAY

Un-Censored

Really insult someone—say something nasty about his or her family!

¡Su abuela!
Your grandmother!

¡Hijo de mala madre!
Bastard!

¡Tu madre!
Your mother!
Wanna be really offensive? Use "su madre," the formal way.

¡Me cago en tu madre!
I shit on your mother!

¡Me chingo a tu hermana!
I @#&! your sister!

Hijoputa. / Hijo de puta.
Son of a bitch.

Esa fue una hijoputada.
That was a shitty move. (Literally: That was a son-of-a-bitchy act.)

 **FOOD**

*F*resh language about food and other delicious goodies.

- ◆ holler about being hungry
- ◆ avoid really gross foods
- ◆ talk about bad eating habits

the big bite

Slang terms for food

A Pepe le gusta mucho...
la comida.
la jama. COSTA RICA, CUBA, ECUADOR, PERU, PUERTO RICO
el morfi. ARGENTINA
la papa. (Literally: the potato) COLOMBIA
el combo. PERU
el papeo. SPAIN

Pepe loves <u>food</u>.

Need some nourishment? Say it!

¡Tengo un hambre!
I'm so hungry!

¡Me estoy muriendo del hambre!
I'm starving!

¡Tengo una sed!
I'm so thirsty!

¡Me estoy muriendo de la sed!
I'm dying of thirst!

¡Tengo antojos!
I have cravings!

Me muero por un helado.
I'm dying for an ice cream.

Some Latino youth consume a lot of fast food, "comidas rápidas"; junk food, "chatarra"; and soft drinks, "gaseosas" or "refrescos". They also love chocolate bars, and there seems to be no age limit to enjoying lollipops. Sport drinks have been all the rage during the past few years. They are the coolest things to serve during house parties as an alternative to alcoholic beverages.

yummy or yucky?

Is that meal good—or gross?

¡Qué delicia! (Literally: What a delight!)
¡Qué ricura! (Literally: What deliciousness!)
¡De rechupete! (Literally: This is scrumptious!) → This is <u>yummy</u>!
¡Uhmmm! (Literally: Mmm!)
¡Ñam, ñam! (Literally: Yummy, yummy!)
¡Ñami! (Literally: Yummy!)

¡Buac!
¡Guácala!
¡Fuchi! / ¡Fo! COLOMBIA → This is <u>yucky</u>!
¡Chish! GUATEMALA
¡Veerga! VENEZUELA

You may or may not want to try some of the most succulent, select dishes in Spain and Latin America: squid in its own ink, octopus in brine, grilled "criadillas" (bull's testicles), cow's tongue in Creole sauce, raw oysters in lemon juice, liver steak, kidney in sauce, oxtail soup, red beans with pork feet, offal casserole... Want more?

overeating

Couldn't eat another bite? Say it!

Tengo una llenura.
I'm so full.

¡Quedé que me exploto!
I'm about to explode!

La comida me cayó como una patada.
The food didn't agree with me. (Literally: The food fell on me like a kick.)

Tengo ganas de...	I feel like...
vomitar.	vomiting.
devolver.	throwing up.
trasbocar.	puking. (Literally: bringing up)

eating habits

Do your friends have poor eating habits? Tell them!

Miguel es un glotón.
Miguel is a glutton.

Carmen come como una vaca.
Carmen eats like a horse. (Literally: Carmen eats like a cow.)

Héctor come como un cerdo.
Héctor eats like a pig.

Carlos come como un pajarito.
Carlos eats like a bird.

Diana es anoréxica / bulímica.
Diana is anorexic / bulimic.

 **PARTYING**

*H*ave a bash in Spanish.

◆ dance the night away
◆ enjoy a little bubbly talk
◆ fire up your language on smoking

dance fever

Dancing is a hot pastime—Latinos are known for their swing and style!

¡Vamos a...esta noche!

parrandear CARIBBEAN

rumbear COLOMBIA

farrear ECUADOR, PARAGUAY

patinar EL SALVADOR

pijinear HONDURAS

chinganear / tonear PERU

tripear VENEZUELA

Let's <u>party</u> tonight!

¿Conoces...?

un buen bar

una buena discoteca

un buen boliche ARGENTINA

un buen antro MEXICO

Do you know...?

a good bar

a good dance club

a good club (Literally: a good bowling alley)

a good dive

Have a good time...

– Vamos a parrandear esta noche. Let's party tonight.

– Buena idea. ¿Conoces una buena discoteca? Good idea. Do you know a good dance club?

– ¡Claro! Sure!

the Scoop

Kids as young as 13 enjoy nightlife in many Latin American countries. At this age, teens party—usually unsupervised—at friend's houses. At around 15 or 16, gals and guys are already going to clubs on their own. By the time they're 18–20, Latin American hipsters are into dance clubs that stay open all night long.

bottoms up!

Just talking about drinks might get you intoxicated!

Esta noche quiero...

beber / tomar.

chupar. CENTRAL AMERICA, BOLIVIA, PERU

mamar. ARGENTINA

escabiar. DOMINICAN REPUBLIC

I want <u>to drink</u> tonight.

Vamos a tomar...

un trago.

un chupi. ARGENTINA

un copete. CHILE

un tapis. EL SALVADOR

unas copiosas / unos chupes. MEXICO

un juanetazo. PUERTO RICO

un cubata. SPAIN

Let's have <u>a drink</u>.

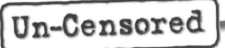

Un-Censored

Slang words can embarrass you if used in the wrong context.
"Chupar" and "mamar" have a sexual connotation: to suck. Anywhere,
except in Argentina and Spain, saying "vamos a tomar un chupi" is
asking for a kiss not a drink. And, if you dare ask for "un copete"
outside Chile—you'd be asking for a fistful of hair. Gross!

Before you drink, make a toast...

¡Salud!
Cheers!

¡A tu salud!
A toast to your health!

¡Fondo blanco!
Bottoms up!

under the influence

Someone's smashed? Every country has its own expression.

¡Manolo está...!
borracho
mamado ARGENTINA, DOMINICAN REPUBLIC
rubio BOLIVIA
curado CHILE
caído de la perra COLOMBIA
socado / socao COSTA RICA
del otro lado CUBA
chumado ECUADOR

Manolo is <u>drunk</u>!

¡Isabel está...!
bola EL SALVADOR, NICARAGUA
a talega GUATEMALA
ahogada MEXICO
en pedo PARAGUAY
choborra PERU
jendi'a PUERTO RICO
ciega SPAIN
aguarapada VENEZUELA

Isabel is <u>drunk</u>!

the scoop

> *What should you be seen drinking on Latin American beaches and other Spanish-speaking hot spots? If you're cool, you'll drink the local alcoholic beverage—aguardiente, rum, tequila, pisco—straight up or with ice, a splash of orange or lemon juice, or a dash of soda. Simple mixed drinks, like vodka or gin with some fruit juice or soda are the standard, as is beer, which is popular everywhere. It's not so cool to drink whisky, wine, or brandy—these are generally considered drinks for older generations.*

one too many

Had a little too much to drink? Wanna talk about someone else who has?

María bebe como una esponja.
María is a heavy drinker. (Literally: María drinks like a sponge.)

Paco ha bebido como bestia.
Paco drinks like a beast.

José anda empinando el codo.
José is drinking [alcohol]. (Literally: José is raising the elbow.)

the day after

Drank too much? Not feeling too well? Share your discomfort.

Tengo...
resaca.
chaki. ARGENTINA
goma. (Literally: rubber) CENTRAL AMERICA
guayabo. (Literally: guava tree) COLOMBIA   I have a <u>hangover</u>.
perra. (Literally: bitch*) ECUADOR
caldero. (Literally: cauldron) PERU
ratón. (Literally: rat) PERU, VENEZUELA

*Not that kind of bitch! This means a female dog.

Suffer the consequences...

– **Javier está muy borracho.** Javier is so drunk.
– **¿Tan rápido?** Already?!

up in smoke

Whether you'd like to light up or want to share your distaste of smoking with those around you, here's the language you need.

¿Tienes un...?

cigarrillo

pucho (Literally: bit) ARGENTINA, CHILE, COLOMBIA

faso ARGENTINA

cáncer (Literally: cancer) PERU

pitillo (Literally: tube) SPAIN

Do you have a <u>cigarette</u>?

¿Te molesta si fumo?
Do you mind if I smoke?

Estás fumando como una chimenea.
You're smoking like a chimney.

Dora fuma como puta encarcelada. ♀ ⚡ COLOMBIA
Dora is a chain smoker. (Literally: Dora smokes like a whore in jail.)

Antonio fuma como un carretero. ♂ SPAIN
Antonio is a chain smoker. (Literally: Antonio smokes like a cart driver.)

¡Deja de fumar!
Stop smoking!

the high life

These expressions are for reference only...

Está...
drogada. (Literally: drugged)
volada. (Literally: flown) CHILE
trabada. (Literally: stuck) COLOMBIA
del otro lado. (Literally: on the other side) CUBA
colgada. (Literally: hung) SPAIN
olía. (Literally: smelling) VENEZUELA

She is <u>into drugs</u>.

Estoy volando.
I'm high.

¡Qué soye! COLOMBIA
What a trip!

No consumo drogas.
I don't do drugs.

busted!

Here comes a section you want to know about but don't want to need.

Me pusieron una multa por...	I got a ticket for...
exceso de velocidad.	speeding.
pasarme la luz roja.	going through a red light.
no hacer un pare / un stop.	rolling through a stop.

Need to get out of a ticket?

Lo siento, no vi la señal.	**¡Soy turista!**
I am sorry, I didn't see the sign.	I'm a tourist!

police watch

Slang terms for cop...

¡Allá viene un...!

cana ARGENTINA, DOMINICAN REPUBLIC, URUGUAY

paco BOLIVIA, CHILE, VENEZUELA

tombo COLOMBIA, COSTA RICA, PERU, VENEZUELA

cuilio EL SALVADOR

chonta / guarura GUATEMALA

chepa HONDURAS

cuico MEXICO

gandul PUERTO RICO

mono / madero SPAIN

Here comes a <u>cop</u>!

behind bars

Who got caught doing what?!

Lo...	He got...
agarraron.	busted.
arrestaron.	arrested.
detuvieron.	detained.
engrillaron. CHILE	shackled.
trancaron. DOMINICAN REPUBLIC	locked up.

Though many Latin American countries have begun to penalize officials who accept bribes, paying someone off is still a common practice to avoid arrest or fines. As a visitor, it's best to avoid making a bribe—trying to buy off an honest official can land you in jail, or worse.

ENTERTAINMENT

*B*ehind-the-scenes language on music, movies, and TV.

- ◆ *chill out and talk about cool tunes*
- ◆ *televise your Latino boob tube lingo*
- ◆ *get the facts on Latino films*

listen up

Get ready to swing your hips and shake your coolie!

Me encanta...	I love...
la música pop.	pop music.
el rock en español.	Latin rock.
el rock clásico.	classic rock.
el vallenato. CARIBBEAN, COLOMBIA	vallenato.
la salsa. CARIBBEAN, COLOMBIA	salsa.
el merengue. CARIBBEAN, CENTRAL AMERICA	merengue.
la cumbia. COLOMBIA, VENEZUELA	cumbia.
la bachata. DOMINICAN REPUBLIC	bachata.

Soy...de la salsa.	I am a salsa...
amante	lover.
fanático	
fana ARGENTINA	fan.
afiebrado COLOMBIA	
fiebrú PUERTO RICO	devotee.

¡El concierto estuvo...!	The concert was...!
buenísimo	so good
espectacular	spectacular
chévere	cool
poderoso CHILE	
la verraquera COLOMBIA	super
a todo dar MEXICO	awesome
de puta madre	great (Literally: of a bitch mother)
de mierda	the shit

Me gusta escuchar música a todo volumen.
I love to hear music at full blast.

necessary equipment

What you need to listen to tunes...

discman
discman

radio
radio

reproductor de MP3
MP3 player

audífonos
headphones

reproductor de CD
CD player

parlantes
speakers

grabador
cassette player

equipo de sonido
sound system

the Scoop

Many young Latinos listen to American pop music, but they also love Latino pop stars. More and more Latino musicians have gained international acclaim, and for good reason—Shakira, Ricky Martin, and Marc Anthony are some of the best examples. You may want to check out some local pop favorites— Alejandro Sanz, Café Tacvba, Ilegales, Juanes, Maná—they may show up on the pop charts sooner than you know it!

tv & movies

Learn some boob tube and show biz slang, then enjoy the show!

Me encanta ver...	I love to watch...
dibujos animados.	cartoons.
telenovelas. (Literally: TV novels)	soap operas.
culebrones. (Literally: snake shows) SPAIN	
noticieros.	the news.
reality shows.	reality shows.
talk shows.	talk shows.

¿Dónde anda la guía?
Where are the TV listings?

Pásame el control.
Give me the remote.

¡No me cambies el canal!
Don't change the channel!

Vamos al cine.
Let's go to the movies.

Vamos a alquilar una película.
Let's rent a movie.

¿Tienen...?	Do you have...?
películas de acción	action movies
comedias	comedies
películas románticas	romance movies
películas de terror	thrillers

¿Está...?	Is it...?
en español	in Spanish
en inglés	in English
subtitulada	subtitled
doblada	dubbed

"Premios TV y Novelas" are top-ranked TV awards shows, equivalent to the Golden Globes, and hosted in Mexico and Colombia—two big giants of TV production in the Spanish-speaking world.

Oscars equivalents are: "Festival de San Sebastián" (Spain), "Festival de Cine de Cartagena" (Colombia; TV awards are also given during this festival), and "Festival Internacional del Nuevo Cine Latinoamericano" (Cuba). These international events are televised in most Spanish-speaking countries.

The renowned music event, "Festival de Viña del Mar" (Chile), recognizes new musical talent every year. The awards party takes place on the beautiful Chilean coastal city of Viña del Mar—a totally rockin' town.

If you like the hot rhythms of the Caribbean, you shouldn't miss the "Festival de Música del Caribe"—the location changes every year, but a beach paradise and dance fever are always guaranteed.

The Latino version of the MTV, Billboard, and Grammy awards are managed and celebrated in the US—they include the cream of the music world from Latin America and Spain. You can catch them on cable TV and on some national channels.

GESTURES

*T*hese Latino gestures are pretty unique! Just remember: even within the Latino community, gestures may have a completely different meaning from region to region. Use with caution.

I forgot!

Along with this gesture, exclaim: **"¡Mierda! ¡Se me olvidó!"** *Shit! I forgot to do that!*

He or she is drunk!

Do this discreetly.

He or she is so cheap.

Used to avoid saying the word **"tacaño"**, *stingy*, which is pretty harsh.

He, she, or it is delicious!

Say, **"Ummmm"**, *mmm*, to reinforce your pleasure.

chapter 14

I want to have sex.

It's subtle, but use it with care—some people might feel offended!

I want to have sex. I had sex. He or she had sex.

Oh! Very suggestive!

He or she is gay.

This is downright nasty and rude—be careful!

In Spain, this is an offensive gesture exclaiming that you want to have sex with someone.

He is masturbating.

Another dirty gesture—don't do it liberally.

We have many gestures in common with Latinos, but here are a few gestures that we don't share...

Don't rub the palms of the hands together if you're cold. This, to a Latino, means that you're excited!

Don't shrug or raise your shoulders to signal I don't know—this is a rude way to show a Latino that you don't care.

Did you just give someone the OK symbol by making a ring with the forefinger and the thumb? It doesn't mean OK—it stands for @#&! you! and is very offensive.